SELF-HYPNOSIS
To
Stop Smoking

By

Herb Marlow, Ph.D.

Introduction

This is a **"Self-Hypnosis to Stop Smoking"** program that always works if the procedures and suggestions are followed. Please don't try to take a shortcut; follow the scripts chronologically through the book and you will find that you can stop your smoking addiction without chemicals or outlandish programs. **"Self-Hypnosis to Stop Smoking"** is not a "quick fix" program. It builds slowly in your subconscious to not help you overcome nicotine addiction. This is a life-style change that has only an upside.

First, Make sure that you are ready to quit smoking. Too often smokers are urged to quit by other people, and that is *not* incentive enough to accomplish your goal. Test yourself and see if you are ready. Do some self-talk and ask yourself why you want to quit smoking. If you find that your personal incentive is strong, then this program will be effective and give you the help you need.

WORDS OF CAUTION! Don't tell people that you are on a "stop smoking" program. When you have stopped completely and the craving is gone forever, then you can say "I used to smoke, but now I don't," or words to that effect. Keep in mind that if you tell others what you are doing while you are doing it, there will be those (usually other smokers) who try to sabotage your plan. I know that sounds irrational, but trust me, it happens.

While you are following the **"Self-Hypnosis to Stop Smoking"** program, if someone offers you a cigarette, take it and say you'll smoke it later. Then, when you are alone you can flush it down the toilet.

I have used the skill set in this book to help many people stop smoking, and it has always worked.

All hypnosis is (basically) self-hypnosis. A rash claim you say? Let me explain.

I began using hypnotherapy in my counseling practice quite a few years ago. I studied under one of the foremost hypnotherapists in the Dallas/Fort Worth Metroplex, who had studied under the father of hypnotherapy Milton Ericson.

My original goal was to find a positive source of therapy for people suffering from short-term and chronic depression outside drug therapy. It seemed to me that since depression was a subconscious psychological disorder, the debility should be treated on a subconscious level without chemicals. After years of practice, hypnotherapy has proven to be as effective in lifting the dark shadow of depression as I had hoped and I have discovered that this form of therapy can successfully treat many more problems than depression.

Here is a partial list of debilities and situations that can be treated by hypnotherapy:

Weight control

Quitting smoking and other tobacco addictions

Relieving depression

Overcoming grief

Raising self-esteem

Treating identity problems

Overcoming drug and alcohol addictions

Relieving anxiety

Anorexia

Bulimia

Each of the above subjects may be addressed in separate books. This volume is all about **Self-Hypnosis to Stop Smoking.**

So what is hypnosis and/or hypnotherapy? Simply put, hypnosis is the gateway into the power of the subconscious mind. Our minds are very powerful. The conscious mind can and does help us function in the everyday world, but the subconscious mind actually controls the conscious mind. In the subconscious is found memory banks that are constantly active. Also, all of the bodily functions are controlled by the subconscious – ever wonder what controls your breathing rate and heart rate? The subconscious mind. That is probably enough of the clinical side, and I'll not expound, but as you continue you will see what I am writing about and be glad you bought this book.

My claim that all hypnosis is really self-hypnosis is built on my own training and practice. In my counseling office, once I have induced a trance in an individual a few times, the subject will self-induce hypnosis the minute he/she sits down in the chair. In an early counseling visit if I ask a person about using hypnotherapy, and that person agrees, then that tells me he/she is open to subconscious psychotherapy through hypnosis – keep in mind that hypnotherapy is psychotherapy administered to a subject under hypnosis.

Can a person be hypnotized against his or her will? Milton Ericson proved that is possible, but no therapy can be accomplished after that kind of induction as there are too many barriers in the mind that cannot be overcome.

Hypnosis is often used in Crisis Counseling to divert (Diversion Therapy) a subject bent on violence and bring peace to a troubled situation. However, that is very different from the type of hypnosis and hypnotherapy than you will learn in this book.

Effective hypnotherapy can only be successful with the subject's approval and acceptance. Since you have purchased this books that tells me that you are ready to learn the techniques necessary to make hypnosis a positive factor in your life.

In the pages of this work you will find self-induction techniques, entry and exit time sets, post hypnotic suggestions for specific issues, and lasting sub-conscious changes. You, the reader will be in control of your own mind as I teach you how to use hypnosis for your benefit. Remember that hypnosis is *not* mind control – that is, it is not someone else controlling your mind. However, it *is your* mind control in that you will be controlling your own mind.

Please put out of your mind hypnosis shows seen on stage or TV. Yes, these actors do use hypnosis, but of a very different variety. Our aim is to use hypnosis as a positive sub-conscious change agent.

Everyone falls naturally into the hypnotic state twice in a 24 hour period without thinking about it. Just as you are falling asleep you will be in a twilight period where you are almost asleep but not quite, and again in the pre-awakening time when you are almost awake but not quite. At these two points each day everyone falls into a hypnotic state. What I am going to teach you in this manual is how to induce these natural hypnotic states in your own mind at any time.

Also, I enjoy feedback, so please feel free to email me at herb@herbmarlowbooks.com with comments, questions or success stories.

Here's to your success in **Self-Hypnosis to Stop Smoking**.

Chapter One

The Beginning

Perhaps you have asked yourself why you ever started smoking in the first place. I know I did. The answers to that question are many and varied, but the end of the tale is that you are now addicted to nicotine. Keep in mind that addictions are always two-fold: psychological and physical.

The physical addiction comes after the psychological addiction, and the two working together is why it is so hard to quit. When my first child was born, a son, I smoked cigarettes and had done so for many years. One afternoon when Jimmy was about a year-and-a-half old I came home from work to find him rolling up small pieces of paper and putting them in his mouth "just like Daddy." That was the incentive for me to stop smoking, but it wasn't easy. I had not studied hypnosis at that time, but looking back I can see that stopping would have been much easier if I had.

Self-determination is a wonderful thing, and backed up with hypnotherapy it changes lives. Using **Self-Hypnosis to Stop Smoking** takes your self-determination to a new level.

Let's begin:

We will start with a relaxation technique, which is the introduction to hypnosis.

It is best to read the following over and over until you have memorized the procedure. That way you will not have to keep referring to the written words. Also, this Relaxation Technique will always be your introduction to **Self-Hypnosis to Stop Smoking.**

In a quiet room by yourself, find a comfortable place to sit – a recliner, a cushioned chair, a couch – close your eyes and relax. Take five deep breaths, letting each one out slowly. Pull a pleasant picture out of your sub-conscious memory into your conscious mind. It is better if this picture is of a landscape with no humans in it. Cattle grazing in a field, or horses in a paddock are okay, but with very little motion. Let the picture become clear in your mind and enjoy looking at it.

Now, take five more slow breaths and feel your relaxation grow. Stay in this relaxed state as long as you wish, and when you are ready, count backwards from three to one and open your eyes.

This is not yet a hypnotic trance, it is a **Relaxation Technique**; it is also a preparation for hypnotherapy. Please memorize the above procedure so that you will not have to read it. For the next two days, practice this relaxation technique as many times a day as possible until it becomes a habit. The amount of time you spend in this relaxation state is not as important as how often you practice. It can be five minutes or ten minutes, or a half hour. You determine that. What you are doing is forming the habit of the relaxation technique. I'm sure you will soon find that you'll look forward to having this quiet time to yourself.

A few words of caution. Always use the technique when you are alone. Make sure there are no interruptions during your relaxation time, but if there is an interruption, take care of it and go back to relaxation. I have had people tell me that in their very active households it is difficult to find a quiet period where they can do the relaxation technique, and I understand. However, this is the preparation to **stop smoking through hypnotherapy,** so work out the kinks before we move into the actual induction for hypnotherapy. (If you can find no other quiet place, a bathroom will work, though it might not be the most comfortable room in the house.)

Now, this suggestion may be difficult to accomplish, but if possible, don't share how you are working on stopping smoking until you are content with your results. Not only are there scoffers behind every tree, but there are actually people who will try to sabotage your efforts for hidden reasons of their own. A quiet demeanor and a closed mouth are good assets for **Self-hypnosis to Stop Smoking**.

Chapter Two

"Your Goal"

There really is only one goal when you use **Self-Hypnosis to Stop Smoking** – that's right: the goal is to stop smoking and never smoke again! Many people try to quit by "cutting down" the number of cigarettes they smoke each day, assuming that they will reach the point where the desire for nicotine will just go away, but that will not work. Perhaps you've tried that mode to stop smoking and discovered that you were fooling yourself.

The only way to stop smoking is to reach a point where you say to yourself: "I'm done! No more smoking from this point forward!" With that kind of determination and the help of self-hypnosis you will quit forever.

Chapter Three

"Beginning Trance"

Please review Chapter One. By now you should be very familiar with the relaxation technique, but if not, please take some time – perhaps a few days – to practice that technique until it becomes a part of your sub-conscious.

I will include the **Relaxation Technique** here in case you need a refresher:

In a quiet room by yourself, find a comfortable place to sit – a recliner, a cushioned chair, a couch – close your eyes and relax. Take five deep breaths, letting each one out slowly. Pull a pleasant picture out of your sub-conscious memory into your conscious mind. It is better if this picture is of a landscape with no humans in it. Cattle grazing in a field, or horses in a paddock are okay, but with very little motion. Let the picture become clear in your mind and enjoy looking at it.

Now, take five more slow breaths and feel your relaxation grow. Stay in this relaxed state as long as you wish, and when you are ready, count backwards from three to one and open your eyes.

HYPNOTHERAPY PROCEDURE

Please memorize the following so that you do not have to read it.

Beginning Trance Technique

Close your eyes again and take five deep breaths, letting each one out slowly, and feeling the relaxation fill your mind and body. Now that you are relaxed, open your eyes and find a spot on the wall (or the ceiling if you are using a recliner) and focus on it.

As you focus on the spot – and it can be any spot – repeat in your mind the words "ten minutes." Do this several times to program your subconscious for a ten minute session. Once you have set the time, still focusing on the spot, take five deep breaths and let them out slowly. You will find as you are taking these breaths that your eyes will want to close – that's fine, let them close on their own. Notice that in your mind you have a picture of the spot you were focusing on. That is very relaxing.

You will now find yourself growing even more relaxed and you will notice your breathing – slowly breathing in and out, in and out, in and out. With each slow even breath you will become more and more relaxed. The spot will remain in your mind as you breathe, and a very peaceful feeling will come over your mind and body. At this point your blood pressure will lower and you will be so relaxed you will feel like you are almost asleep. Enjoy this feeling until your mind tells you that the preset time of ten minutes is up and you will slowly open your eyes and feel very comfortable.

You may now go about your daily tasks, but the feeling of peace and contentment will be available to you at all times. If you feel stress or have negative feelings, or a desire for nicotine, simply close your eyes and take one deep breath and the picture and peace will return.

Whenever you are alone for a few minutes in a private place, close your eyes and take five deep breaths, and then breathe normally. Let your sub-conscious mind feed the trance technique to your conscious mind, and enjoy the relaxed feeling.

We will now move on to a deeper trance.

Chapter Four

"Deep Trance Technique"

Please memorize the following so that you do not have to read it. Once you have followed the **Relaxation Technique**, and the beginning **Trance Technique** you are ready for a deeper trance. Become comfortable and follow the instructions below.

Deeper Trance Technique

As you are sitting relaxed with your eyes closed, repeat in your mind the words "thirty minutes" several times. This is programming your subconscious mind for how long you want the session to last. Once you have set the time, take five deep breaths and let them out slowly. Now, pull that picture from the relaxation technique into your conscious mind and focus on it. Notice particular parts of the picture, even to seeing small branches on the trees and the blades of grass. Take your time and see the picture clearly from this aspect.

You will now find yourself growing even more relaxed and you will notice your breathing – slowly breathe in and out, in and out, in and out. With each slow even breath you will become more and more relaxed. The picture will remain in your mind as you breathe, and a very peaceful feeling will come over your mind and body. At this point your blood pressure will be lower and you will be so relaxed you will feel like you are almost asleep.

Now, slowly open your eyes and find a spot on the ceiling if you are lying down or in a recliner, or a spot on the wall if you are sitting up. Focus on that spot until your eyes grow heavy, and let them close.

Enjoy this feeling until your mind tells you that the preset time of thirty minutes is up and you will slowly open your eyes and feel very comfortable.

You can now go about your daily tasks but the feeling of peace and contentment will be available to you at all times. If you are stressed or have negative feelings, any time you close your eyes and take a deep breath the picture and peace will return.

Practice this trance technique for several hours or days until it becomes second nature to you. In fact, you will find that after while just closing your eyes and breathing deeply will induce hypnosis. That's good. Now we'll take the next step.

Chapter Five

"Post-Hypnotic Suggestions"

Now that you have learned to induce self-hypnosis, it is time to begin setting post-hypnotic suggestions to stop smoking. You will re-program your mind to change your behavior and desires about smoking.

You will notice that up to this point I have not suggested that you avoid cigarettes or count the hours between smokes. That's because all of these things will be brought under control as you follow the program.

It would be ideal to say don't be around other people who are smoking while working on the **Self-Hypnosis to Stop Smoking** program, but that may not be possible. If not, please don't worry about it. As you work on the program second hand smoke or other people smoking will not make you want to smoke. However, as we continue with post-hypnotic suggestions, cigarette smoke from others will become offensive to you and you will want to get away as soon as possible.

You will also notice that I have not suggested that you throw all of your cigarettes and other smoking paraphernalia (pipes, tobacco pouches, etc.) away. If that is helpful for you, get rid of those things. However, if you have made up your mind to stop smoking – if you are determined to quit for yourself and not at the suggestion of or pressure from others, those items will not deter you.

The first post-hypnotic suggestion is about the desire to smoke. Please memorize these post-hypnotic words as you will be using them shortly and you don't want to have to rely on reading them:

"When I feel the desire to smoke I will close my eyes, take five deep breaths and let them out slowly. Then in my mind's eye I will see myself grinding a cigarette out in a large ashtray. As I am putting the cigarette out I will experience the smell of a skunk. When the cigarette is completely out, the skunk smell will disappear."

Repeat this simple phrase until it is memorized. If memorization is a problem for you, write the phrase out on a piece of paper several times in a row. That will always aid memorization.

Now, Make yourself comfortable and begin the relaxation technique:

In a quiet room by yourself, find a comfortable place to sit – a recliner, a cushioned chair, a couch – close your eyes and relax. Take five deep breaths, letting each one out slowly. Pull a pleasant picture out of your sub-conscious memory into your conscious mind. It is better if this picture is of a landscape with no humans in it. Cattle grazing in a field, or horses in a paddock are okay, but with very little motion. Let the picture become clear in your mind and enjoy looking at it.

Take five more slow breaths and feel your relaxation grow.

Now, follow the **Beginning Trance Technique**: (Please memorize so that you do not have to read.)

As you are sitting relaxed with your eyes closed, repeat in your mind the words "thirty minutes" several times. Once you have set the time, take five deep breaths and let them out slowly. Now, pull that picture from the relaxation technique into your conscious mind and focus on it. Notice particular parts of the picture, even to seeing small branches on the trees and the blades of grass. Take your time and see the picture clearly from this aspect.

Now that you are relaxing, open your eyes and find a spot on the wall (or ceiling if you are using a recliner) and focus on it. As you focus on the spot – and it can be any spot – repeat in your mind the words "thirty minutes." Once you have set the time, still focusing on the spot, take five deep breaths and let them out slowly. You will find as you are taking these breaths that your eyes will want to close – that's fine, let them close on their own. Notice that in your mind you have a picture of the spot you were focusing on. That is very relaxing.

You will now find yourself growing even more relaxed and you will notice your breathing – slowly breathing in and out, in and out, in and out. With each slow even breath you will become more and more relaxed. The spot will remain in your mind as you breathe, and a very peaceful feeling will come over your mind and body. At this point your blood pressure will lower and you will be so relaxed you will feel like you are almost asleep.

Now add:

"When I feel the desire to smoke I will close my eyes, take five deep breaths and let them out slowly. Then in my mind's eye I will see myself grinding a cigarette out in a large ashtray. As I am putting the cigarette out I will experience the smell of a skunk. When the cigarette is completely out, the skunk smell will disappear."

Speak slowly either aloud or silently over and over until you feel the nudge of the set time ending. At the time limit you will slowly come back and enjoy continued peace.

This procedure is designed to program your sub-conscious with the idea of curbing your desire to smoke. Practice it for several days in a row, as many times a day as you can. You will find very quickly that you will not want a cigarette nearly as often as you did, and if you do light one, it will smell like a skunk and you will want to put it out completely.

Chapter Six

"The Post-Hypnotic Suggestion to Quit Entirely"

Since the sub-conscious is the seat of all addictions, desires and hungers, it is also where great positive changes can take place. Often we hear of people that have overcome some problem – perhaps a long term problem – by self-determination, and we applaud those people, but not all of us can do that without help.

Since you have now mastered self-hypnosis, it is time to use that vehicle to stop smoking and withdraw completely from your nicotine habit. We have already done the preparation for this program in limiting your desire to smoke. You are also committed to stop smoking forever. Now we will reinforce your commitment.

Make sure that you have followed the post-hypnotic suggestion in Chapter Five long enough to develop the skunk smell in your sub-conscious mind. If you are unsure, repeat the trance induction and the process until you feel confident. (The skunk smell has no magic in it – if you smell something else obnoxious, that's okay. Use that smell. Some of my subjects use the smell of a dirty diaper and it works as well as the skunk smell.)

Now you will go into a deep trance for the final post-hypnotic suggestion. This trance is a bit different than, and builds on, the one you used earlier. You will need to be in a room that is completely isolated for this procedure will take one hour. Again, memorize the following procedure so that you will not need to read it.

DEEP TRANCE TECHNIQUE

In a quiet room by yourself, sit in your favorite chair, or lie back on your favorite couch, close your eyes and relax. Take five deep breaths, letting each one out slowly. Pull the pleasant picture out of your sub-conscious memory into your conscious mind. Let this picture become clear in your mind and enjoy looking at it.

Now, take five more slow breaths and feel your relaxation grow.

You are now very relaxed with your eyes closed, repeat in your mind the words "one hour" several times. Once you have set the time, take five deep breaths and let them out slowly. Now, pull that picture from the relaxation technique into your conscious mind and focus on it. Notice particular parts of the picture, even to seeing small branches on the trees and the blades of grass. Take your time and see the picture clearly from this aspect. Breathe it in with each breath you take.

You will now find yourself growing even more relaxed and you will notice your breathing – slowly breathing in and out, in and out, in and out. With each slow even breath you will become more and more relaxed. The picture will remain in your mind as you breathe, and an even more peaceful feeling will come over your mind and body. At this point your blood pressure will lower and you will be so relaxed you will feel like you are almost asleep.

Now that you are relaxing, open your eyes and find a spot on the wall (or ceiling if you are using a recliner or couch) and focus on it. As you focus on the spot – and it can be any spot – repeat in your mind the words "one hour." Once you have set the time, still focusing on the spot, take five deep breaths and let them out slowly. You will find as you are taking these breaths that your eyes will want to close – that's fine, let them close on their own. Notice that in your mind you have a picture of the spot you were focusing on. That is very relaxing.

Let a picture of your face with a cigarette in your mouth come into your mind. The cigarette is burning, about half-smoked. Inspect this picture carefully. As you are looking at it you will notice your eyes squinting as the smoke is floating up into your face. This smoke will irritate your eyes and the smell of a skunk will be present.

Now you begin to feel nauseous. The smoke and skunk smell bring on the nauseous feeling. Watch as you remove the cigarette from your mouth and put it out in a large ashtray. Once the cigarette is completely out, the skunk smell and the nauseous feeling will go away.

Repeat this procedure until your mind tells you one hour has passed. Then you will open your eyes and still feel relaxed – **and you will not want to smoke!**

You must find a time and place to follow this procedure for an uninterrupted one hour period. Use the procedure several times a day – particularly when you feel any small desire to smoke. Keep in mind that you are progressively changing you subconscious mind to reject smoking. Repetition is the key. The more you repeat the procedure, the stronger it will become in your mind.

Chapter Seven

Post Hypnotic Suggestion Reinforcement

Below you will find a shortened version of the one-hour trance – please don't use this version until you have instilled the longer one in your mind. If you try, it will not work. This procedure is built upon all the previous work you have done.

After you have used the deep one-hour procedure enough times you will find that a shorter version will work for quick, short-term reinforcement. Our sub-conscious minds constantly turn things over and reform them, and that is true of hypnotic trances and suggestions.

By this time in the program you have settled in your sub-conscious the following:

The Relaxation Technique

The Beginning Trance Technique

The Deep Trance Technique

The Post-Hypnotic Suggestion Technique

Now that you are an experienced hypnotic subject you have graduated to the advanced class.

Throughout every day or evening you may come in contact with other people's smoke and it may cause discomfort to you.

I don't mean the discomfort of desiring to smoke, but rather the discomfort of nausea. The following short technique will help you in those situations.

Following is a short cut to **Self-Hypnosis to Stop Smoking.**

Find a place where you can be alone for a few seconds or minutes (Perhaps a restroom or supply room.) Close your eyes and bring the image of the spot into your conscious mind. Focus on the spot and breathe deeply five times. As you do, the image of putting a cigarette out in the large ashtray will become clear. You will also experience the skunk smell and slight nausea. Open you eyes again and the smell and nausea will go away.

You can now go on with your normal duties and activities, knowing that at any time you can repeat the short cut procedure. You can actually do this in a crowded room if necessary by un-focusing your eyes and take the five deep breaths.

Please allow me to repeat here: this program is a long term change in your sub-conscious mind from craving nicotine to overcoming the desire to smoke. If you follow the procedures in the book **SELF-HYPNOSIS TO STOP SMOKING** will work and you will never want to smoke again.

Chapter Eight

"Conclusion"

You are now a student of self-hypnosis. That does not mean that you have the skills or power to hypnotize other people, but it does mean that you have unlocked the door to your own subconscious. The more you use the procedures in this book, the better you will feel. Also, since self-hypnosis is a positive life-style change, as you lose your desire to smoke, you will see the benefit in changing other habits, negative feelings and actions.

Good luck with **"Self-Hypnosis to Stop Smoking."**

Dr. Herb Marlow
herb@herbmarlowbooks.com

www.ingramcontent.com/pod-product-compliance
Lightning Source LLC
Chambersburg PA
CBHW051429250726
48655CB00003B/1315